IMPROMPTU MAGIC
WITH PATTER

BY

GEORGE DeLAWRENCE

With an Introduction by
A. M. WILSON, M.D.

Illustrated by
HARLAN TARBELL

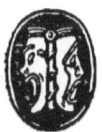

British Library Cataloguing-in-Publication Data
A catalogue record for this book is available from
the British Library

A Brief Introduction to
Magic Tricks

Magic is a performing art that entertains audiences by staging tricks, or creating illusions of a seemingly impossible, or supernatural nature – *utilising natural means*. These feats are called magic tricks, effects, or illusions. Some performers may also be referred to by names reflecting the type of magical effects they present, such as *prestidigitators* (sleight of hand), *conjurors* (purportedly invoking deities or spirits), *hypnotists* (involving individuals mental states), *mentalists* (demonstrating highly evolved mental abilities) or *escape artists* (the art of escaping from restraints or traps). The term 'magic' is etymologically derived from the Greek word *mageia*. Greeks and Persians had been at war for centuries and the Persian priests, called *magosh* in Persian, came to be known as *magoi* in Greek; a term which eventually referred to any foreign, unorthodox or illegitimate ritual practice.

Performances which modern observers would recognize as conjuring have probably been practiced throughout history. But for much of magic's history, magicians have been associated with the devil and the occult. During the nineteenth and twentieth centuries, many performers capitalised on this notion in their advertisements and shows. In the UK, this association dates back to Reginald Scott's *The Discoverie of Witchcraft*, published in 1584, in which he attempted to show that witches did not exist, by exposing how many (apparently miraculous) feats of magic were done. The book is often deemed the first textbook about conjuring, but all obtainable copies were burned on the accession of James I in 1603, and those remaining are now very rare. For many centuries, magic was performed either on the street as a type of entertainment for the common masses or at court, for nobility. During the early 1800s however, large-scale magic performances began making their way onto the theatre stage. Modern entertainment magic owes much to Jean Eugène Robert-Houdin (1805–1871), originally a clockmaker, who opened a magic theatre in Paris in the 1840s. His speciality was the construction of mechanical automata which appeared to move and act as if they were alive; a feat which wowed his audiences for many years.

The escapologist and magician, Harry Houdini took his stage name from Robert-Houdin and developed a range of stage magic tricks, many of them based on what became known after his death as 'escapology'. Houdini was genuinely skilled in techniques such as lock picking and escaping straitjackets, but also made full use of the range of conjuring techniques, including fake equipment and collusion with individuals in the audience. In the modern day, these forms of magic easily transferred from theatrical venues to television specials; a transition which has opened up myriad new opportunities for deceptions. It has also brought stage magic to vast audiences, as most television magicians perform before a live audience, who provide the remote viewer with a reassurance that the illusions are not obtained with post-production visual effects. Some modern illusionists believe that it is unethical to give a performance that claims to be anything other than a clever and skilful deception. Most of these performers therefore eschew the term 'magician' (which they view as making a claim to supernatural power) in favour of 'illusionist' and similar descriptions. On the other side of the coin, many performers say that magical acts, as a form of theatre, need no more of a disclaimer than any play or film; this viewpoint is reflected in the words of magician and mentalist Joseph Dunninger, who stated that 'for those who believe, no explanation is necessary; for those who do not believe, no explanation will suffice.'

Although there is also discussion among magicians about how a given effect should be categorised, they broadly fall into the following categories: 'Production' (where the magician produces something from nothing; a rabbit from a hat for example), 'Vanish' (where something disappears), 'Transformation' (where a silk handkerchief may change colour), 'Restoration' (where the magician will destroy an object, then restore it to its original state, 'Teleportation' (where a borrowed ring may be found inside a ball of wool, or a canary inside a light bulb), 'Levitation' (where the magician, or some person or object defies gravity), and 'Prediction' (where events are predicted under seemingly impossible and unexplainable circumstances).

IMPROMPTU MAGIC
WITH PATTER

CONTENTS.

IMPROMPTU MAGIC
WITH PATTER

INTRODUCTION

Nature is not alone in abhorring a vacuum. The literature of magic is sadly lacking in the initiatory stage of the foundation principles of the simple deceptions that really deceive without apparently doing so.

At the dinner table, the parlor gathering, the impromptu meeting of friends at a neighbor's, do you know of any book or pamphlet on magic that fills the bill?

Well, IMPROMPTU MAGIC, WITH PATTER, does that very thing, and does it satisfactorily. The author, George DeLawrence, has been a society entertainer for many years, has learned the in's and out's of the whims and exacting demands of social affairs, and knows how to meet them with just the thing that fills the gap and prevents the ennui of what promised to be a dull time at the gathering satiated with music, song and cards. Magic is an art that sometimes instructs, often amuses and *always entertains*.

The Commercial Traveler, the Book Agent, the Insurance Solicitor, in fact any man who finds it difficult to interest a "prospect," will find many things in this book that will help to land a sale or secure an order. For the first principle in dealing with another is to gain attention and arouse interest. Nothing will accomplish this end quicker than

will an impromptu trick, done with seeming uncon-
sciousness of having done anything.

Many books and booklets on patter, numerous
works, little and big, on magic, have been published.
But not until this work of DeLawrence has there
been one that covered both, and with material that
anyone of reasonable intelligence could use success-
fully and satisfactorily.

Having read the manuscript I congratulate the
author on his wise selection of tricks and on the
sensible and appropriate patter accompanying them.
The fortunate purchaser is also to be congratulated,
for he will have a veritable mine and inexhaustible
storehouse of material that will prove a boon and
blessing in time of need, and thus will be able to
prove himself an entertainer who actually entertains.

A. M. Wilson, M. D.

IMPROMPTU MAGIC
WITH PATTER

AUTHOR'S PREFACE

You will pardon, I trust, this somewhat lengthy preface to IMPROMPTU MAGIC, WITH PATTER. In covering a field that has been sadly neglected by most writers on magic and sleight-of-hand, this detail has been gone into for your own benefit, that at the end of the book you not only may know how the various tricks are accomplished, but will be able to present them yourself.

The author as a boy was naturally backward, due mostly to fact that he could neither sing, play a musical instrument, nor otherwise "perform." Hence at social gatherings he was, more or less, what is termed a "wallflower." Chance brought a copy of a magic dealer's catalogue into his hands. He invested in some apparatus and spent long hours in secret practice, with the result that thereafter he had a diversion to offer at parties and various social gatherings; and, instead of remaining a "wallflower," he became a much talked-of entertainer.

I realize that many young people are in the same position today. Magic is an art that is always interesting, will make you a welcome guest at any social function, and, with proper practice, may also be the means of your earning a fair recompense as an entertainer. Therefore this book of off-hand tricks—with complete explanations and instructions, illustrations of the various moves, and the necessary

9

"patter," or talk to cover—has been prepared for your benefit.

First, I am going to tell you the basis of all magic, be it the smallest pocket trick or the largest stage illusion. That is misdirection; in other words, deceiving the eye into believing it sees certain things which actually are not so. The hand is not quicker than the eye, but it can easily deceive that optic. For illustration: Take a coin in the left hand, place it once or twice in the right hand, then, instead of placing it in the right hand, retain it in the left, dropping this hand carelessly to your side, while the right hand closes the fingers as if containing the coin and is raised above your head. Every eye will follow the right hand. That is your deception, the basis of magic; or, as I have termed it, misdirection.

A word as to practice. Even the most simple tricks should be practiced several times until you are sure of yourself, so that you can go right ahead and perform the trick without hesitating or fumbling. The difference between the raw performer and finished performer is this: The former does not know what he is going to do, while the latter knows just what he is going to do. There are no tricks explained here that require any degree of trained dexterity, or more than an hour's practice. Considering that card and coin experts and other exponents of the art of magic spend years in practice, you will appreciate more the value of the tricks or effects explained herein, some of which are even more startling than those requiring considerable skill.

You have, no doubt, often noticed an amateur magician who perhaps was able to accomplish the work he set out to do, but made a miserable attempt in his presentation talk, or what the professional calls "patter." This is the hardest and most difficult part of his "turn" or "act." It has proved the stumbling block for more than one aspiring and otherwise clever magician. So I have added this feature, a short, snappy talk to cover each trick, in order that, after you have learned the moves of execution, you may at once be in position to present the effect before a gathering and present it in a manner that will be a credit to you.

Half the battle is won when you know you are right, for then nervousness and "stage fright" should be of short duration. However, don't lose hope if you get nervous the first two or three times you endeavor to work before an audience. Even the most hardened professional went through the same agony, and this bugaboo sometimes returns to haunt him in later years, such as on opening nights, or at the first presentation of a new act.

While this volume of simplified magic is intended for the beginner who wishes to achieve sleight-of-hand effects without being obliged to spend much time in study and practice, it is hoped that the book will be of interest and value to my fellow professionals as well.

IMPROMPTU MAGIC
WITH PATTER

THE POSSESSED MATCH HEAD.

Three heads of paper matches appear in this trick, or in lieu thereof, three pieces of dough, or bits of rolled-up tissue paper. To the spectators, three heads are used. In reality you have four heads, one being concealed at the base of the fingers on the right hand, between the first and the second fingers.

The heads are laid on the table. Then one is picked up by the right hand and placed in the left, which immediately closes, thereby keeping the match head from view. A second head is likewise picked up by the right hand, and, when placing it in left, the concealed head is allowed to drop with it into the left hand which immediately closes as before. Three heads are now in the left hand, which the audience thinks contains but two.

Pick up the third and last head from the table with the right hand. You apparently throw it under the table or off to one side, but in reality this head is held between first and second fingers near their tips, the thumb aiding in getting it into this position.

The match heads in the left hand are thrown on the table, showing three therein, and making it appear that the discarded head has joined the first two in the left hand.

You can repeat the operation, actually throwing away the last head this time. Then, if you desire to repeat again, have concealed in the wrinkles of the

13

trousers, above the knees (if seated at table), one or two similar match heads, which can be easily obtained by the right hand as the left throws the three heads out on the table.

The Patter:

I have here, ladies and gentlemen, three little match heads, which you see are very ordinary, no strings, threads nor magnets being attached.   I want you to count them carefully—one (*place in left hand*), two (*place in left hand*), and here is number three, which we will discard under the table. (*Throw away*.)   But strange to say, it hops right back to its friends, and here we have one, two, three. (*Throw on table*.)   For the benefit of those who were not paying attention, I will once more demonstrate this painless operation. Three match heads; number one; here is number two, and number three goes on the floor. But before you can wink an eyelash, here he is—three. Mr. ———— seems skeptical, so to convince him that it is not the contents of any bottle that causes this match to hop, here goes again. Number one; here is number two, and number three actually is thrown across the room, but instantly— here he is. One, two, three.

THE PENETRATING MATCH.

Either matches or toothpicks can be used in this experiment. The toothpicks are better, as there is less solid matter to grasp between the fingers. If the picks are too long, break them off to a size that can be easily handled.

The effect is as follows: A toothpick is held between the first finger and the thumb of both the right and the left hands. Then, bringing the hands quickly together, they are caused apparently to pass through each other, being interlocked as shown in Figure 1.

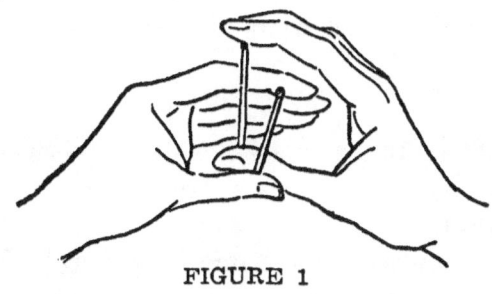

FIGURE 1

The secret is: The toothpick in the right hand is not held between the thumb and first finger alone, but is grasped by the first and second fingers so that it can be held by these fingers when the thumb is drawn away. You make two motions of the hands, bringing them close together, and on the third motion, release the thumb of the right hand, bringing the toothpick a short distance away from the thumb, as in Figure 2, the free end going down inside of the stick

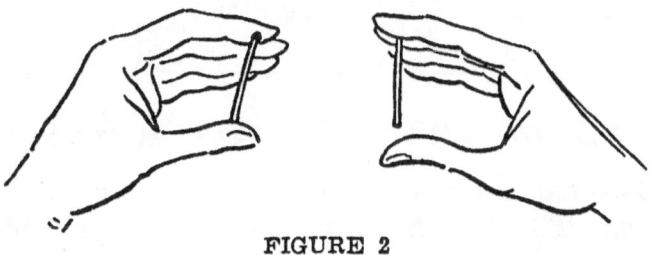

FIGURE 2

held in the left hand. The instant they have passed the thumb comes against the free end, as in Figure 1, causing a perfect optical illusion.

It will take several minutes' practice to get the movements down so that the hands work in harmony, but when this is accomplished with the hands in motion, the bringing away of the thumb cannot be seen even under a spectator's very eyes.

To bring the toothpick out, simply reverse the movements, finishing with the hands separated a foot or more.

The Patter:

An after-dinner dessert—toothpicks—generally furnished by chop houses free of charge. (*Show toothpicks.*)

You will notice I have one in my right hand; also one in my only remaining hand. Nothing peculiar about that. However, what I am going to do is very peculiar; something that was shown to me by an old Indian, Prince Bon Ami by name.

By moving the hands quickly together, on the third movement one toothpick, invisibly and without leaving a trace, penetrates the other—like that. It's a poor rule that won't work both ways. So when you desire to get the toothpick out, simply reverse your count—three, two, one—and there, the dirty work is done. (*Repeat if desired.*)

THE DISAPPEARING MATCH HEADS.

Two flat paper matches are exhibited in the right hand. The left hand passes over them and the heads disappear. Another motion and they again appear, in both cases the two sides being shown with or without heads, as the case may be.

The actual operation is caused, in the first in-

stance, by previously shaving off the head on one
side of each match. To show both sides with heads,
hold the matches between first finger and thumb about
level with your waist, so that the shaved sides of
the matches cannot be seen. Then bring the hand
upward with a quick motion, at the same time giving
the matches one turn sidewise by rolling them between your fingers. The upward motion should be
made with an inward curve, so that when the hand
stops the heads of the matches are pointing toward
the body. Thus, while you have appeared to turn
the matches over but once, you have given them also
a sideways turn, so the same side appears to view as
at first, and the under side is again out of sight. You
have apparently shown both sides of an ordinary
match. Now bring the hands back down to the first
position, again twisting the matches between the fingers, and the heads are again in view. To cause the
heads to disappear, pass the left hand over the
matches, and under this cover give them a side turn
with the right hand, bringing the shaved sides to
view. The upward movement may be made without
turning the matches, if it is desired to show the
opposite side. It will be seen that by following
these movements the matches may be shown at will,
either with or without heads.

The same trick may be done with paper matches
which have printing on one side, making them appear
plain or printed on both sides.

The patter is written for this effect.

The Patter:

Most of you are familiar with the shrewdness of the
Hebrew race and what wonderful salesmen they are.

The other day I witnessed the most clever piece of selling ability that so far has come to my notice.

This salesman was selling matches—ordinary paper matches like these two. He was explaining to his customers the advantage of advertising, saying his firm would print his ad on one side of the match, as is customary with these articles. Another person standing by spoke up and said: "Vell, I vould puy some of your matches, but I vant my ad on both sides." The salesman, nothing daunted, said: "That's easy, just pass your hands over these matches, and there you are. Advertising on this side, also on the reverse side." Another fellow butted in, saying: "I could use some, but I don't want any advertising at all." Up spoke the salesman again: "That's the beauty of our matches. If you want the match to be entirely blank, pass the hand in the other direction. Nothing on this side, likewise nothing on this side." The first customer spoke up: "That is certainly a most wonderful match, but for myself, I'd like to have the advertising on one side." "Fair enough," said the salesman. "Move the hand downward, and there is your wish. An ad on this side, the other perfectly blank." I might say that he sold a heap of matches.

THE PENETRATING QUARTER.

This is to be performed while seated at a table.

To get the best effect, three quarters or half dollars are used. One quarter is concealed in the palm of the right hand, which in conjuring parlance is termed "palming." It will be found a simple matter to hold a quarter in the hand without cramping it to a noticeable degree. The two visible quarters are laid on the table, about five or six inches from the edge. The performer picks up one coin with the right hand, which holds the palmed coin, of course not allowing the palm of the hand to be seen. The right hand is placed under the table and the left at the same time picks up the remaining coin. Now take this last coin, snap it down on the table and keep it covered with the fingers of the left hand, while the right hand under the table drops the quarter from finger tips into palm, causing the two to click. Bring up the right hand with the two quarters and throw them out on the table. At the same time the left hand, with a quick but natural jerk, snaps the coin off the table, allowing it to drop into your lap. You have apparently caused one quarter to pass down through the table top, joining the one previously held there.

If you experience any difficulty in palming the quarter, place it, unknown to the audience, on your knee instead of palming it. Go through the above routine, picking up quarter on your knee when the right hand goes under the table, and drop it into the palm at the right moment.

The Patter:

Here is a little trick shown me by a Chinese friend of mine, my laundryman; by name, Wun Bum Lung. When I saw it performed it was done with Chinese coins—"cash," I believe they call them. I started to buy some, but found the freight on two-bits' worth amounted to $11.34, so I experimented with quarters and finally accomplished the seemingly impossible.

This Chink took two coins and laid them on the

table, as I am doing. Then he picked up one and
held it under the table, right below the remaining
coin, which he took and snapped like this. At the
same time he sang out: "Chow, Chow, Chow Mein."
And—would you believe it? The coin penetrated the
table. When he brought out his right hand the two
were together, just like that. Marvelous, isn't it?

COIN AND GLASS OF WATER.

This effect requires a little skill, but the biggest as-
set is plenty of nerve.

The effect: A dime or other small coin is placed
on the table, a playing card laid over it, and this in
turn covered by a fedora or soft hat. The audience
is asked which shall appear, heads or tails?

No matter which the choice may be, the hat and
card are lifted and the experiment is then tried again.
You will probably fail, so you say you will cause the
coin to pass through the top of the table. Then when
the hat is lifted your audience sees on the table, instead of the coin, a glass partly filled with water.

This is performed while you stand at a small
table, with the audience standing all around you, and
here is where the value of misdirection is appreciated.

Just before you perform this trick, secretly procure an ordinary drinking glass and fill it, half-way
or a little more, with water or any other liquid. Then
place the glass under the vest so that its base rests
against the top of the trousers. The glass will easily
stay in this position and you need have no fear of
dropping it out, nor is the bulge noticeable.

Borrow a soft hat and lay it on the table. Borrow a coin and place it on the table and cover it

with a card. Over these place the hat and ask someone to call "heads" or "tails." Generally the request
will be opposite to what appeared when the coin was
placed. Lift the hat with the right hand, bringing it
to a natural position against the body at the waistline, where the glass reposes. Have someone lift
the card. If the coin is not as called for, say that
something went wrong, and make excuses; or if correct, say you will try it again anyway, and repeat the
covering and uncovering with card and hat. Once
more bring the hat to the waist line. When the
party starts to lift the card, all eyes are naturally
focused on the table, and this gives you ample opportunity to secure the glass with your left hand,
place underneath the hat and grasp it with the right
hand through the top of the hat, all unnoticed.

This time take up the coin with the left hand, and
lay hat and glass on the table. Do not drop it so as
to make a noise, but dent in the top of the hat if
necessary to hold the glass. The coin in the left hand
is apparently placed in the right which at once makes
a throwing motion under the table. Lift the hat with
your left hand and there is your glass of water, on
the table. This trick is sure to cause a lot of surprise and favorable comment.

The Patter:

I was talking the other day to a magician who
showed me what wonderful control he had over coins.
So this evening, for your edification, it is with pleasure I repeat one given me in strict confidence.

Will some soft gentleman lend me his hat? Pardon
me, I mean will some gentleman lend me a soft hat?
Any kind at all. This one is entirely satisfactory.

My next request is going to be harder to grant. Someone please let me have a dime. Yes, I'll give it back.
I thank you. The dime I will place on the table, covering it with the playing card (*or a calling card will
answer the purpose*), over which goes the hat.

Now, then, if you will tell me which you desire,
heads or tails, the coin will obey my command and
appear in that position. Heads? Heads it shall be.
(*Lift up the hat yourself.*) Kindly raise the card.
Heads, that is correct. Once more, you will notice it
is now heads. Over it goes the card, and then the
hat. What is your pleasure this time? Tails? Very
well, tails it shall be. Please lift the card. (*Get your
glass of water.*) What is it? Heads? Something
went wrong this time, I fear. I'll try it in a different
manner, causing the coin to pass up through the table.
What do you want this time? Heads? Very well, it
must be heads. Lift the hat and see if I am not correct. (*The glass of water is found, which concludes
the experiment.*)

THE TRAVELLING COINS.

This is based on the principle of the old cups and
balls and the three-shell game.

The effect: Four nickels or pennies are placed
seven or eight inches apart in the form of a square on
a cloth-covered table as in Figure 3.

Two playing cards or other similar pieces of stiff
paper are placed over coins one and two. Coin three
is taken in the right hand and apparently pushed up
through the table. On lifting the card that was
over coin one, two coins are found there, as in the
arrangement shown in Figure 4. Coin four is next

taken and likewise appears to penetrate the table, so that three coins assemble in number one position. The

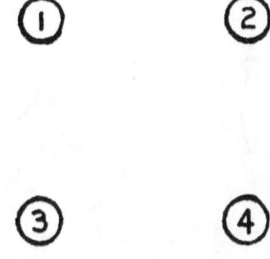

FIGURE 3

last coin is then caused invisibly to congregate with the others, all four being found finally under the first card.

The method: The four coins are placed first as shown in the diagram; two cards are exhibited, one

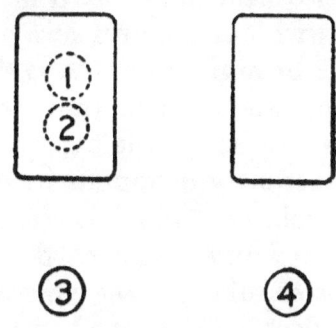

FIGURE 4

being held in each hand. Cover coins one and two, calling attention to the fact that two coins are covered and that two remain in view. Now lift the cards from coins one and two, and cover coins number three and four. Then move the cards back from three to one and from four to two, but as you place the card over coin two the right hand picks up the coin and holds it with the tips of the fingers against the underside of the card. (Figure 5 shows the method.)

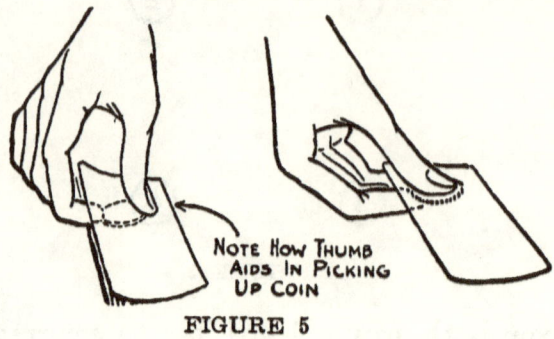

NOTE HOW THUMB
AIDS IN PICKING
UP COIN

FIGURE 5

Practice these moves until they can be made without awkwardness. Do not look at the right hand when executing the move.

With coin two held under card in the right hand, the left hand, with card, moves away from coin number one, and is brought over the right hand so that it exactly covers the card in that hand. The right hand with coin two under the card then moves away, the left hand instantly dropping its card and apparently covering coin two, which is really held under the card in the right hand. This card in the right hand is now placed over coin one, the concealed coin two being allowed to drop as the card touches the table, but care should be taken to see that the two coins do not hit each other, which would cause them to "talk."

Your audience is now under the impression that a coin reposes under each card, while actually coins one and two are in number one position, while there is no coin in number two position. (See again Figure 4.)

Now openly pick up coin three with the right hand

and place it underneath the table. During this move drop it into the left hand, which is also held below the level of the table. The right hand under the table snaps its finger against the wood and is brought out empty. Pick up the card in number one position with the right hand, while the left hand below the table is getting the coin to the tips of the first and second fingers. When the card in number one position is lifted, two coins are shown to be under it, and the card is then passed from the right hand to the left, which takes the card, keeping the coin concealed thereunder. With the left hand the card is replaced in number one position, the third coin being dropped, secretly, alongside of the other two.

Repeat the same operation with coin four, which will apparently bring three coins in position number one, whereas four are actually in that spot. Tap the card in position two, lift and show that the fourth coin has disappeared and has joined the others under the card in position number one.

The Patter:

Most of you are familiar with these coins—nickels or "jitneys"—but I am going to convince you that they are possessed of peculiar characteristics. Making a square of the round nickels I will again call your attention to the fact that there are four—four and no more; also that these are two very ordinary playing cards. By covering these two coins, two are still in sight. Likewise if I cover these two, the former are in view. No matter which two are hidden, two always remain where you can keep your eyes on them.

I will take this coin, place it under the table and cause it to instantly and invisibly pass right through said table and join the coin already there. Of course some of you are undoubtedly skeptical, but you see I'm telling the truth. Two coins are really there. I'll try it again, and want you to keep your eyes on me very closely. Here is the coin. Under the table it goes—one, two, three—and here it is with the other two, leaving one more coin under this card. But to show you how square and fair I am, this coin will be caused to vanish and join the others right in plain sight. (*Tap the card.*) It has already done so, as I presume most of you are aware, for you see here are the four coins all together.

FOUR COIN TRICK.

The effect: A penny is placed in the palm of the right hand and another in the left hand. The hands are then closed, and palms turned upward. One of the audience lays another penny on the ends of the closed fingers of each hand. With a throwing mo-

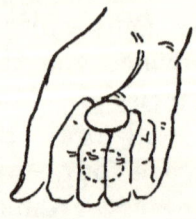
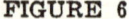
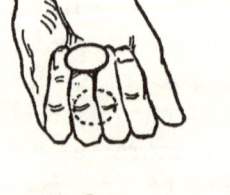

FIGURE 6

tion, and turning the hands downward, one penny is caused to transfer, invisibly, to the other hand, so that the left hand, when opened, is found to contain three coins, and but one remains in the right.

The method: Four pennies, or similar coins, are placed as described and shown in Figure 6. When the hands are turned over the left hand opens and grasps the outside penny with the finger tips, so that the two are held in that closed hand. But when the right hand turns, it opens and drops on the table the penny in the palm as well as the one on the finger tips, so that the coins are located as shown in Figure 7.

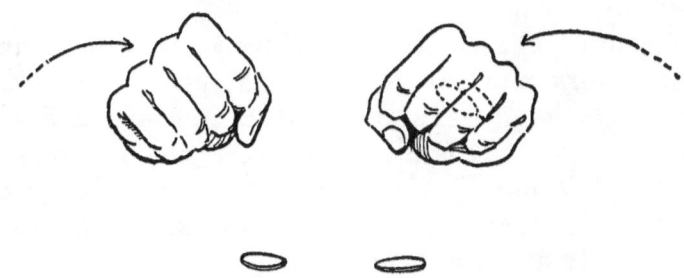

FIGURE 7

To the audience it now appears that the pennies which rested on the finger tips of both hands fell on the table. Remark that the trick did not work, and again request one of the audience to place the pennies on the finger tips as before. Hold the hands far apart and quickly turn them over, opening the fingers sufficiently to grasp the coins with the finger tips and pull them inside the fists. When the hands are now opened the left hand holds three coins and the right hand one, yet the audience has not seen how the coin was passed from one hand to the other.

The Patter:

Ladies and gentlemen, this is a cheap trick. I use pennies—four of them—thereby making it a four-cent trick.

One penny I will place in my right hand and one in my left hand, which is half the trick. The other two pennies I wish you would place on the ends of my fingers, one on each hand. I thank you.

Watch me closely, and remember: The closer you watch the less you see. (*Turn hands and drop coins.*) Pardon me, my mistake. It didn't work that time. Would you mind replacing the pennies once more on my finger tips?

Again. Watch closer. (*Turn.*) It is done, and I doubt very much if you saw that penny travel from the right hand to the left. But, anyway, as Shakespeare says: "It is did." There is the one lone cent (*open left hand*), the other little rascal being over here where there was more cents (*open right hand*). It's really a nonsensical trick.

COINS OUT OF HAT.

Use four, five or more coins, of the same denomination but with different dates. Place them all in a hat and mix them up. Turn your back, requesting that a coin be removed, the date noted, and the coin then replaced in the hat. You take out the coins one at a time and hand over the selected one.

The secret is very simple. When a coin is removed from the hat and held in the hand it becomes warm. You can easily pick out the warm coin from the others, which will feel cold in comparison. Pick the coins from the hat one at a time, until you feel the warm one. This ingenious little trick can be repeated many times without fear of detection.

The Patter:

I would like to get a half-dozen or more nickels (*or quarters*) of different dates. I want to convince you that the influence I hold over coins is genuine. By the way, the coins will be returned to you in a few moments.

We will place them all together in a hat and mix them up. While I turn my back I will ask Mrs. ——— to remove one of those coins from the hat. Hold it tightly, so I cannot see it in any way. You have the coin all right? Now look at the date quickly. You have observed the date? Then drop it into the hat and shake it to mix up the coins. (*Begin picking up the coins and when you feel the warm one, stop.*) Do you remember the date of the coin you looked at Mrs. ———? This is it—the one you chose. Just try it again, and I will convince you that my picking out the chosen coin was not an accident.

THE HAUNTED COIN.

This is, in a way, a spiritualistic effect, patterned after the rapping hand, which answered questions through the code of spiritism; that is, rapping once for "yes," twice for "no," and three times for "doubtful" or "I do not know." It requires some secret preparation, but the resultant fun is worth the trouble.

Procure an ordinary drinking glass. Place in it a metal washer to which is tied a length of black silk thread. Cut a piece of writing paper in a circular disk slightly larger than the top of the glass, punch a small hole in the center, and run the end of the thread through this hole. Paste the paper on the top of the glass, which will prevent the washer from being pulled out. The glass can then be placed inside the trousers at the back, or a special holder can be made to secure it there. It may be fastened to the back

of the trousers at the waist.   By jerking the thread
the washer can be caused to rattle in the glass, answering questions with one, two, or three clinks
or   rattles,   as   desired.   To   work   the   washer
any   of   the   following   three   methods   may   be
adopted.   First: Run   the   free   end   of   the
thread off to an assistant, who at the right moment
pulls the thread; or, second: Run it down into right-
hand trousers pocket, with the end fastened to a
piece of cardboard, in order that the thread can be

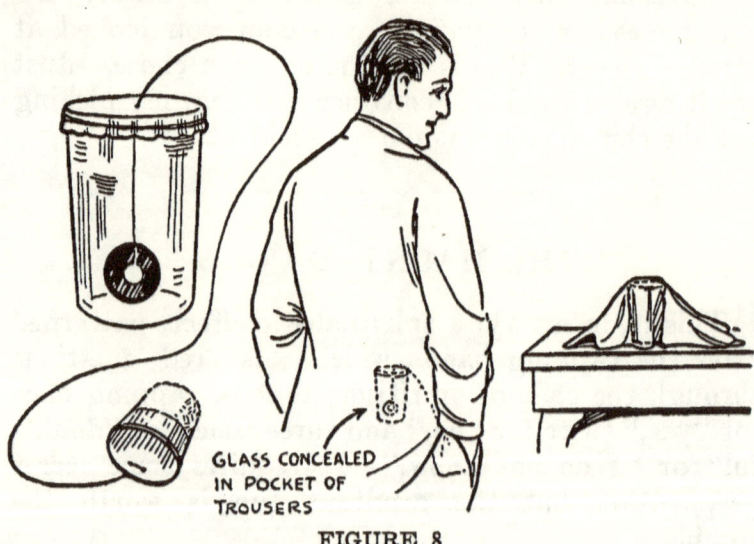

GLASS CONCEALED
IN POCKET OF
TROUSERS

FIGURE 8

easily found and will not get away from you.   In
this case it is necessary to work with your hand in
your pocket; or, third: Use a thimble painted black,
to which is soldered a small hook, allowing the thimble to be attached to trouser leg, the thread being
tied to the hook, as in Figure 8. When the proper
time arrives the finger can be inserted in the thimble,
and by a slight movement of the hand the necessary

raps or rattles are caused. The thread will have to be measured to fit the working method that you prefer.

The trick is worked as follows: A glass and a coin are borrowed or picked up from the table, the coin is thrown in the glass, and the glass is then covered with a handkerchief. Various questions are asked, and the effect is that the coin in the unprepared glass rattles the answer.

This is best worked when seated at a table. But, if you are standing, see that you are at one end of the room with the audience all in front of you.

The coin in the glass being covered with a handkerchief, the fact that it does not move is unknown to your audience, as is the presence of the concealed glass and coin. They hear the coin behind you, but they naturally assume that it is the coin in the glass in your hand, which necessarily is held perfectly still to preclude a suspicion that the rattle is caused by your jerking the glass.

A similar experiment can be made by having the glass fastened to the back of a piano, etc., a string leading off into another room where your assistant is located. Of course you should keep the displayed glass in close proximity to the hidden glass, so that the noise comes from the proper locality.

The Patter:

Often have I witnessed the feats of various spiritualists, especially their supposed communication with some astral personage. Generally these manifestations took place in the dark, or the knocks were received on a table some distance away. But I am going to give you a demonstration along these lines, here in this room, with you in close proximity to me.

There shall be no darkness, and the articles are very ordinary ones—a small glass, a coin and a handkerchief, and I'm ready for work.

If anybody would like to ask questions I will endeavor to have my control, "Bull Durham," answer for you, using the regular code in vogue with spiritualists. That is, one rattle for "yes," two for "no," and three rattles for "I do not know," or "doubtful."

(*Endeavor to be humorous, and if persons are backward in asking questions, make them up yourself. For instance, pick out some young unmarried lady.*) Is this lady married? (*Two rattles.*) No. Would she like to be married? (*One rattle.*) Yes. In the near future? (*One rattle.*) Yes. How many children will she have? (*Keep on rattling a dozen times or so. Go on asking questions, and answer them as meets the situation.*)

DIME AND PENNY TRICK.

The effect: A person places a dime in his hand and closes it tightly. You offer to bet that the dime is there, or that it is not there. Have him open his hand and the dime still remains. Try it again. This

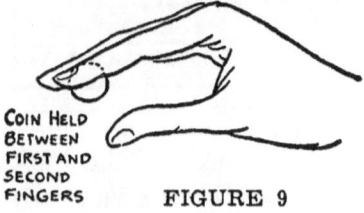

COIN HELD
BETWEEN
FIRST AND
SECOND
FINGERS   FIGURE 9

time he will probably be willing to bet almost anything that the dime is grasped tightly in his fist, but on opening it, instead of a dime a penny is found.

The customary method for performing this effect requires skill and hard practice, but it has been simplified herein so that anyone, with a little patience and an hour or two of practice, can procure the same result as when more difficult sleights are performed.

The method. At the start of your experiment you secretly have a penny grasped between the tips of the first and second fingers, as in Figure 9, just enough of the penny being grasped by the fingers to insure its being held. The hand is always kept with the palm down, or with the palm toward yourself, so that the presence of the penny will not be noticed. Borrow a dime from your prospective victim, taking it in the hand other than the one containing the penny. Transfer it to the latter hand, taking it with the tips of first finger and thumb.

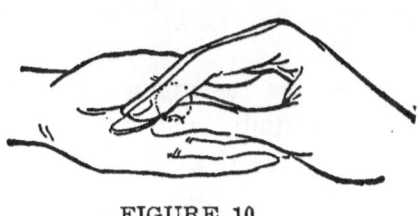

FIGURE 10

Request him to open his hand, lay the dime therein, making this move after the manner shown in Figure 10, and immediately cover it with the thumb of the hand holding the penny. Ask him to close his hand. See Figure 11.

When he has done this, draw out your thumb. Inquire if he thinks he still has the dime. Then ask him to open his hand. Of course the dime is still there. Pick up the dime and request that his hand be dried.

Here you exchange the dime for the penny. This is the only hard part of the trick, and these moves should be carefully practiced. When he starts to wipe his hand, pick up the dime with your hand containing the penny, taking it with the tips of first finger and thumb. Move the thumb up over the dime, drawing

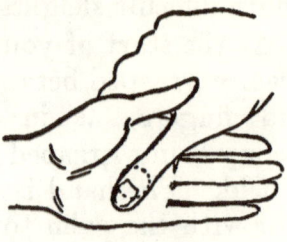

FIGURE 11

it along the first finger until it gets past the concealed penny, then allowing it to drop into the palm of the hand. The thumb comes back over the penny, covering it from view, and the "switch" has been made.

The penny is now resting against the first finger, covered with the thumb, just where you held the dime a moment ago. Place it in the palm of your friend's

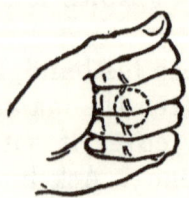

FIGURE 12

hand, all the time keeping it from view and immediately requesting that his hand be closed. As you previously placed a dime therein, and as he thinks your intention is to get the coin away from him, he will naturally think the dime is in his hand because he feels a coin there (Figure 12).

Unless of a very skeptical or knowing nature, he will undoubtedly bet anything under the sun that he still has the dime in his hand. The author has worked this trick a thousand or more times and can safely say that over ninety per cent of the victims "bit." The fact that they may be aware of an old trick similar to this, but worked differently, will also add to the surprise.

The Patter:

This is a slick dime and sometimes it's "slicker." I want to show you a little experiment—one that you can try out on the wife when you get home.

Kindly hold out your hand, and I will place the dime in the middle of your palm. Close your hand around my thumb. That's right—but not quite so tight. Leave me a little room to work. Here we go —one, two, three (*jerk out thumb*). Would you be willing to bet, sir, that you still have the dime? I wouldn't want to take your money. And to tell the truth, I sometimes fail. Just open your hand. You still have it, I see. Your hand is a little moist. Would you mind wiping it with your handkerchief? (*Pick up dime and make "switch."*) That is better. Again, close your hand over the dime. Are you ready? Once again—one, two, three. This time will you bet you still have the dime? (*You can work up the discussion as much as the occasion permits, and then*:) Well, I know you're mistaken. Let me see the dime. (*He finds a penny, not a dime, and you win.*)

THE RED, THE WHITE OR THE BLUE.

The effect: Three paper washers or discs with holes in the center of each—one red, one white and

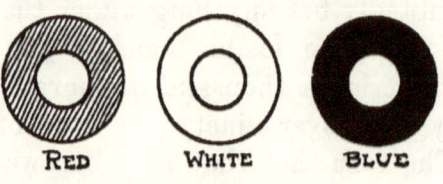

FIGURE 13

one blue—are shown, and are strung on a piece of ordinary twine. One end of the twine is given to some member of the audience and the opposite end to another. The performer places a handkerchief over the washers, hiding them from view (see Figure 14),

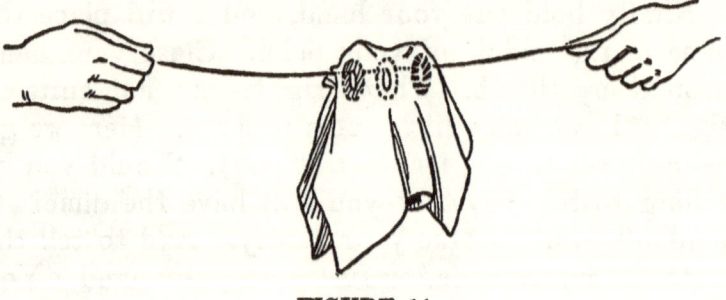

FIGURE 14

and requests that one of the colors be freely selected. Placing his hand underneath the handkerchief, he removes and brings out this colored washer, which is not mutilated in any way, and only two washers of the remaining colors are found on the string.

The method: The three paper washers are threaded in an ordinary manner. There are no false turns of the string, and each party actually holds one end. When the performer reaches in his pocket to get his handkerchief he takes out, at the same time, three similar paper washers, concealing them in the palm of his hand. These washers in the pocket are in a known order as to color. For instance, red one on top, white in the middle and blue underneath. Before covering the three on the string, he makes a mental note of the relative positions of the three colors. Now, when a color is chosen, all the performer does is to pull off this desired one from the string under cover of the handkerchief, conceal it in his hand and push up the duplicate washer of the same color, which he shows as the one removed. When the handkerchief is taken off, the unused duplicates and the torn washer can be placed in the pocket at the same time the handkerchief is stowed away. The trick is easy, but the effect is puzzling.

The Patter:

With your approval, ladies and gentlemen, I am going to show you something that will cause you to think an escape artist is present. I call it "The Mystery of the Paper Washers," or "How Does He Do It?" Here are three paper washers. For the benefit of those who are color-blind I will say that this one is red, this one blue and the third white—colors I know you are all familiar with. Exhibit number two is a piece of twine such as is used to wrap packages. Don't misunderstand me—not a package like the husbands brought home from the club. These three washers I shall thread on a string, asking that you hold one end, and you the opposite end, which is the only one left. Over goes the handkerchief, for two reasons. The spirits won't work without darkness; and, secondly—also the main reason—I don't want you to see how I do it.

Somebody please select one of those colors. Red? Red it shall be. Here it is, the red washer, which you will find is not damaged in the slightest degree. Remaining on the string, of course, are the white and blue washers. Thank you. But—you fellows holding the string—don't tell the rest how it is done.

SWALLOWING A KNIFE.

This little illusion should be performed while seated at a table, with a napkin on your lap to prevent the knife falling to the floor. I would not advocate its exhibition where ladies are present, but this is left to your own judgment.

The effect: The performer places an ordinary dinner knife so that it rests in his two hands as shown in

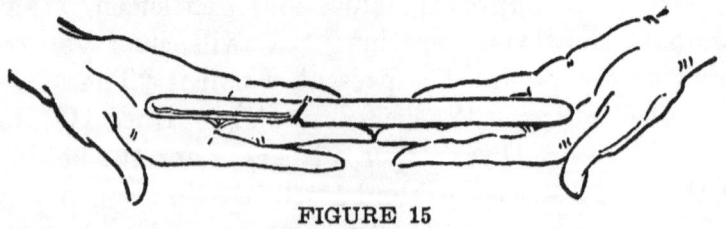

FIGURE 15

Figure 15. The point is placed in his mouth, and the knife apparently is completely swallowed.

The method: The first time the knife is placed to the mouth the performer makes a wry face as though he were afraid to try it. He lowers his hands level with the table. Slightly tipping them toward himself he allows the knife to fall into his lap. The hands are kept in exactly the same position as at first and are immediately placed again to the mouth and drawn on down past it, which creates a perfect illusion of a knife being dropped down the throat.

Do not look toward your hands when dropping the knife into the lap. Correctly presented, your facial contortions will misdirect your observers and the "get-away" is easy.

This effect is performed without patter.

THE DISAPPEARING GLASS.

This is another experiment performed while seated at the dining room table.

Lay a coin at the edge of the table; place over it a plain drinking glass, mouth down, and around the glass twist a piece of newspaper, turning it tightly at the top so that it makes a close-fitting shell over the glass.

Inquire as to what the coin shall be, heads or tails, and pick up the glass and paper to see whether it has obeyed the command. When removing the paper-covered glass draw it toward yourself to the edge of the table, and allow the glass to drop into your lap. The paper will keep the shape of the glass and can be placed down over the coin as before. Once more inquire the desire of the audience as to which side of the coin shall appear. Of course you will fail to cause a change. So you suddenly slap your hand down smartly on the paper, crushing it to the table. The host or hostess will probably draw a quick breath, and the disappearance of the glass will be a complete surprise. The glass can later be produced from under your coat.

The Patter:

Do you mind, madam, if I use this drinking glass? It is all right with you in case something unforeseen happens? Here is an insignificant penny, with your drinking glass as a covering. For the glass, to prevent any deception, I shall make a covering also, using this piece of newspaper. Everything is in readiness. What shall that coin be, heads or tails? Heads, you say? (*Remove glass.*) What is that? My luck has deserted me. Once more I shall try it—with, I hope, better luck. (*Place paper shell over coin.*) What is your pleasure this time? You still want heads? You have me again. No luck! (*Smash paper.*)

TORN AND RESTORED PAPER NAPKIN.

The effect: After tearing a small paper napkin into several strips it is wadded into a ball and, when unrolled, is found entirely restored. You volunteer to show how it is done, but the spectators are none the wiser after you have explained.

Secretly prepare your table as follows: Roll up a paper napkin into a compact ball, which we will call "A," and over this spread another paper napkin which we will call "B," so that "A" is under the corner of "B" that will be picked up by the right hand. At one side have a third napkin, "C," spread out, to one corner of which you have pasted still another rolled-up napkin, "D." You can place on your table a book, a cigar box, or any other article back of which you can drop the torn pieces, as hereafter explained. Have a pencil, to be used as a wand, lying on the book.

Start the experiment by picking up "A" and "B," secretly getting "A" into the palm of the right hand so that the third and little fingers can curl around it and yet leave the first and second fingers free to perform various movements.

Exhibit napkin "B" by holding it out in front of you, while you have "A" hidden in the right palm, as shown in Figure 16. Then tear "B" into several strips,

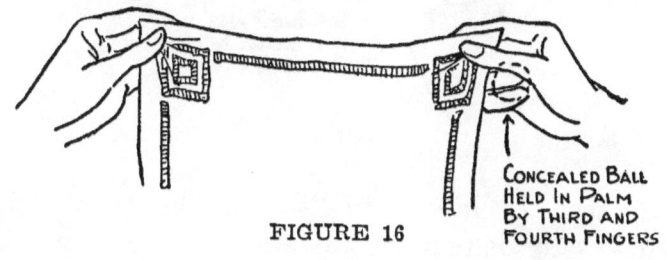

CONCEALED BALL
HELD IN PALM
BY THIRD AND
FOURTH FINGERS

FIGURE 16

and roll them up into a little wad, using both hands. As you appear to squeeze the wad more compactly, it is an easy matter to exchange the two balls under the cover of the hands, so that the torn pieces of "B" go into hiding in the palm and the whole napkin "A" replaces it in view at your finger tips. Pick up your pencil from the book, at the same time secretly dropping behind the book the torn wad "B." While attention is focused on "A," which is held with your left finger tips, pick up the pencil with your right hand, at the same time secretly dropping behind the book the torn wad "B." Wave the pencil over "A," replace the pencil on the book, slowly unroll "A," and the napkin appears to have been restored.

Now you pretend to explain how you did it. Take "A" and roll it into a ball, while you explain about hiding an extra napkin, and openly place "A" in the left palm. Then pick up "C" by the corner to which "D" is attached, and tear it into several strips, always taking care that the presence of "D" is not revealed, and allowing "D" to remain on the last torn strip of "C." Bunch the torn pieces together with the "D," so the audience thinks you simply have a wad of torn strips, as is shown in Figure 17. Under cover of the

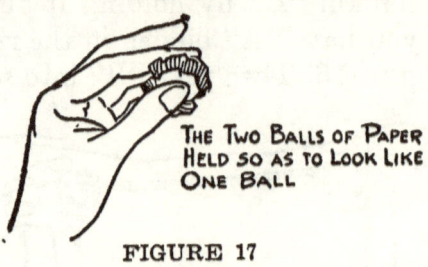

THE TWO BALLS OF PAPER
HELD SO AS TO LOOK LIKE
ONE BALL

FIGURE 17

hands, secretly loosen "D" from the torn strips, which is easily done if the paste is not too heavy. Then secretly palm the torn bits of "C" in the right hand, substituting "D" at the finger tips.

Pretend to show how the exchange is made, openly substituting "A" for "D" so that "D" goes into palm of left hand. Apparently you have exchanged the torn napkin for a whole one. In reality you exchange one whole one for another whole one, while the torn bits are hidden in the left hand.

In reaching for your pencil, secretly drop the torn pieces of "C" just as you got rid of "B" the first time. Wave your wand over "A" which is held at the finger tips, then open "A" and show the napkin restored, which is just what the audience expected. Finally take "D" from the left palm and show that it also is a whole napkin, which is not at all what the audience expected, so you have fooled them again.

The Patter:

This is a Chinese trick. It is called Chinese because you use a Chinese paper napkin, like this. If you do it with a Japanese napkin, it is a Japanese trick. But in reality it is the invention of a South African head-hunter. I call it a ripping trick, because I rip or tear the napkin into a number of strips or bits—two bits, four bits, and some small change—which I will proceed to ball up or roll into a ball. Sometimes I even ball up the trick. After getting this into an almost perfect sphere, I take my pencil, and wave it slowly over the torn scraps. Then, strange as it may seem, on unrolling it we find the little napkin wholly restored.

I will admit that that was a rather foolish trick. Nothing to it, in fact. So I'll show you how to do it. Then you can go home and put one over on your mother-in-law.

The napkin is very ordinary (*show napkin "C"*). Also, I really tore it up and rolled it into a ball. But here is where the dirty work comes in. All the time I had another whole napkin rolled up and concealed here between my fingers. (*Roll "A" and put in left hand.*) But of course I always kept the back of my hand toward you, so you thought it was empty. Then, when rolling it around I quickly changed the torn pieces for the whole napkin. Using a pencil for a magic wand (*reach for it and drop "C"*) is all bunk, but it looks professional. Of course, after I waved the pencil it was a simple matter to unroll the whole napkin. (*Unroll "A".*) These pieces (*showing "D"*) you can get rid of anyway you want. Sometimes they watch me too closely, and if you try it and find that that is the case, simply take the little ball of

torn-up napkin, blow gently thereon, like this, and
pronounce the words "Chow-Mein-Soo." Surpris-
ing as it may seem, if you slowly unroll the ball of
pieces you will find that they have all joined together
(*unroll "D"*), making a complete napkin, just as
good as at the start.

THOUGHT FORETOLD.

This effect might be classified as a so-called psychic
test. It is a trick used by spiritists and those en-
gaged in what is commonly termed "thought transmission." It is an effect never before published in
a book. If presented properly it will make a decided
hit with any audience.

The effect: The performer exhibits a small envelope and a card. The audience sees him write
several items, which he does not show. He then seals
the card in the envelope. Various persons are freely
chosen, or volunteers are called for, to assist the
performer, who requests that they concentrate their
thought when they are told to do so. They are asked
to choose various words, which the performer says
will be found already written on the card. At the
conclusion of the test the card is removed from the
envelope and the performer's statements are verified.
He has apparently foretold their thoughts.

Use an envelope about the size of a number two
drug envelope, or other small size. To the face of
the envelope, on the inside, you have secretly pasted a
piece of red, non-smut, typewriter carbon paper, with
the carbon side down, or facing the bottom of the envelope. It should be short enough to allow the edge

of the envelope to be removed without exposing the carbon paper.

The envelope is held aloft in the left hand, the inside not being shown, but the blank card is freely passed for examination. Take from your pocket a red pencil and pretend to write upon the card, shielding it from the view of the audience as you write. In reality you do not write upon the card at all, but just make a pretense of so doing. Then insert the card, still blank, but apparently written on. The envelope is now sealed and held in the left hand.

When the audience choose the words you make a note of each by writing them down on a loose slip of paper as they are called out. For convenience in writing, use a heavy piece of cardboard, or a memorandum pad, slightly larger than the envelope, as a support.

After sealing the envelope lay it, with card side undermost, on the pad. Over the envelope lay a loose slip of paper for taking notes, so that the envelope rests under the memorandum slip apparently by accident. In making the verification on memorandum pad use a number three black lead pencil.

As you write on the light paper with the hard pencil this writing is transferred in red to the card enclosed in the envelope. So that while you are writing a certain item on the paper, apparently just for verification, at the same time you are also transferring it to the blank card. See that you keep within the space of the envelope, and do not run your writing together on the card in the envelope. At the conclusion of the test lay the paper on the table, open the envelope and hand the card to one of the audience. You retain the envelope, which is crushed between the hands and dropped carelessly into your pocket.

The Patter:

Ladies and gentlemen: For your amusement and entertainment I would like to show you a test in psychic phenomena, demonstrating that such a thing as "thought transmission" actually exists, and that under proper conditions it is obtainable amongst any of us. The only stipulation made is that you remain silent, in order not to disturb the subconscious minds of those taking part in the test.

Here are a small envelope and a plain blank card. On this card, unknown to any of you, I shall write certain things, sealing the card in the envelope. (*Pretend to write, and seal card in envelope.*) I assure you there is not a person in the room who knows what is written on the card, outside of myself. To remove any vestige of doubt or suspicion of trickery any persons you name shall be used in this experiment. Please select three among you to assist me. (*After selecting.*) Thank you.

Mrs. ———, on the card sealed in the envelope I wrote a number between one and one thousand. Will you kindly concentrate your mind for a moment, and when I say "Ready," give me the first number that you happen to think of. All right. Concentrate. Ready! (*Suppose "sixty-six" is given you.*) Sixty-six, Mrs. ———? I see the conditions are very good. You thought of just the number I desired you to; the number written on the card in the envelope. Please keep that in mind. And as a further means of verification I will also jot it down on a slip of paper. Sixty-six. That's right.

Now Mrs. ———, on this card I also wrote one of the cardinal colors. I want you to concentrate for a second. All right. When I say "Ready" tell me the first color that comes into your mind. Ready! Blue? Very fine. Just what I wanted you to think of. Just what I wrote on the card, and which I will verify later on.

Mrs. ————, I will take you last. On this card is also written one of the twelve months of the year. Will you, like the others, kindly concentrate, and when I say "Ready," give me the month you first think of? All right. Ready? June! Just what I thought you would say, Mrs. ————. Just what I wanted you to say. Because it is written on the card.

Mrs. ————, you gave me sixty-six. Mrs. ————, you named blue; and Mrs. ————, June was the month you thought of. Here they are on this memorandum slip as I took them down, and also I will prove to you that they are the identical words I caused you to think of; the ones that at the start I wrote on this card. (*Open envelope.*)

Kindly take the card, Madam. What is written at the top? "Sixty-six." And you gave me that number, Mrs. ————. On my slip I have "blue," as being the color Mrs. ———— thought of. Isn't that the color written on the card? Yes, that is correct. For the last item my slip shows "June," which is the month named by you, Mrs. ————, is it not? Correct. And what did I write on my card, Madam? "June?"

It is a simple matter, when you work with me and follow the instructions given, to cause you to think along just the lines I desire, isn't it?

PARLOR MIND READING.

Here is a very amusing routine for parlor presentation and one that will make you a decided attraction for the evening. It requires the assistance of your wife, your sweetheart or some male friend, and the secret collusion of one guest.

You pass out a number of envelopes and some light-weight blank cards, requesting members of the audience to write any question they desire, sign their name thereto, and seal the cards in the envelopes. Of course one of these envelopes is given to the person who is to secretly assist you, and he or she writes some question that you have already agreed upon, so that you are from the first aware of the contents of one of the envelopes.

While the people are writing their questions, blindfold your assistant with a handkerchief and place her at a table at one end of the room, so that the audience will be in front of you. Amongst professionals it is a well known fact that a bandage over the eyes, while not allowing of sight straight ahead, will nevertheless allow a person to see down the side of the nose. So your assistant can read without difficulty anything placed near the edge of the table.

Collect the envelopes from the writers, taking care that the known one is either collected last or kept on the bottom of the heap. The envelopes are now placed on the table, near your assistant. Pick up the top one, the contents of which you do not know, hold it over your assistant's head and request that she answer the question. She immediately gives a roundabout answer to the question previously agreed upon, which was written by the guest in the secret, and which is now at the bottom of the heap. When the answer is given you ask the person whose name is quoted if that answers her or his question, at the same time tearing open the envelope and apparently reading therefrom the question just answered. In reality you are quoting the question at the bottom of the heap of envelopes, and secretly reading and memorizing the one held in your hand.

Take this card, which you have apparently just read aloud, and carelessly lay it on the table, but see that it is within your assistant's range of vision. She secretly reads the message while you pick up the next envelope and hold over her head, and then she answers it. You tear open this second message, quoting the one on table and memorizing the contents of one held in your hand. Thus you are always one question ahead, and when you come to the final message it will actually be the first one answered, though you give a reply to the one just previously laid on the table. You start your patter as follows:

"Ladies and gentlemen: Undoubtedly at some time or other you have all witnessed a mind reading act; the thought of one person conveyed to another one at some distance; or the reading of sealed messages by mental concentration on the part of the persons concerned. My wife and I discovered, a short time ago, that it was sometimes possible for us to receive impressions strongly concentrated upon by other persons present. Therefore, in order that you may keep the matter in your mind more firmly, I will ask that you write upon these pieces of paper any questions you wish, sign your names thereto and seal in the envelopes which I will also distribute for your use. "The reasons for writing the questions are these: That by so doing they will be more firmly impressed upon your memory. And I then have the written verification, and you will know that I am actually answering a question as propounded by various ones present.

"While you are sealing your questions I will blind-fold Mrs. ———, so that it will be impossible for her to see and at the same time will allow her to center her thought entirely upon the questions that you are thinking of.

"Kindly hand me your questions. Please concentrate intently for a few seconds upon what you have written, which will greatly promote the success of our experiment. (*Collect the sealed envelopes.*)

"Very well, Madam. Concentrate, and answer the question which I hold over your head."

Your assistant answers along these lines: "Let me see. It is a woman asking a question. She wants to know if her husband is going to buy her that new fur. Mrs. Smith is asking the question. Isn't that right, Mrs. Smith? Yes, it will take a little coaxing but you will get it eventually."

Never read the question direct. This savors of trickery, while leading up to it indirectly is more apt to create the idea of mental impressions being received. The direct reading of a question would tend to lead your audience to a suspicion that you had seen the message, whereas the contrary is desired.

You now tear open the envelope, look at the card removed therefrom, and pretend to read the question which is actually in the envelope at the bottom of the heap, and which you know is, "Will my husband buy me that new fur?" (*Signed*) "Mrs.Smith." Place this card, which you appear to have just read aloud, on the table where your assistant can read it. You should memorize it in order that you need not again glance at the table. But you can safely steal a glance should you forget the message.

Proceed with second envelope, answering the question which actually lies on the table, and so on, throughout the entire series. In your answers, endeavor to be entertaining and always give a reply that is pleasing to the writer, for this will accord you a better reception than in the case of depressing or negative replies.

UNSIGHT, UNSEEN.

To the average audience the following card effect appears to be a feat of divination. It is one of the few tricks that can be repeated several times with continued mystifying results.

The effect: The performer lays twenty-eight cards face upward on the table, in four rows of seven cards each. He turns his back to the cards and requests some person to think of any one of the fifty-two cards in the pack. When the card has been mentally chosen he inquires in which row on the table there is a card of the same denomination as that of the card thought of. Upon receipt of this information he asks the suit of the card selected. Thereupon, without again looking at the cards on the table, he immediately names the card thought of.

The method: The four rows contain cards of certain denominations which should be previously arranged so that they can be dealt out in this order, or at least so that the given cards appear in a given row, irrespective of the sequence. The four rows should contain cards of the denominations shown in Figure 18.

Each row has a "key" number. The key to the first row is "one"; the second row is "two"; the third row is "four," and the fourth row is "eight." To illustrate the use of these key numbers, we will assume that an ace has been chosen. You are told that

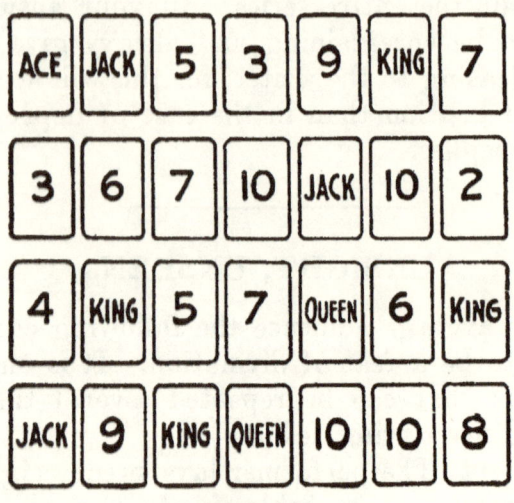

FIGURE 18

it appears in the first row only. The key is "one." Hence it must be one or an ace. If they chose a seven, they will report it in the first, second and third rows. You add the key numbers. "One" plus "two" plus "four" equals seven. The jack is considered as eleven, the queen as twelve, and the king as thirteen.

In order to memorize the arrangement so that the cards may be placed in order at any time without resorting to the diagram, just remember that the first row starts with "one" and the numbers alternate, thus:

1—3—5—7—9—11—13.

The second row has "two" as the key card, and the cards run in alternate pairs, as follows:

2, 3, —, —, 6, 7, —, —, 10, 11, 10.

Only six cards are required in this row, so an extra ten is added to fill the gap.

For the third row the key is "four." The first card is a four and they run four consecutive numbers, then skip four, thus:

4, 5, 6, 7, —, —, —, —, Q, K, K.

Only six cards are needed in this row so an extra king is added to fill in.

In the fourth or last row the key is "eight." The cards start with an eight and run consecutively, with an extra ten added, as the consecutive run ends with a king. So the cards in the last row are:

8, 9, 10, 11, 12, 13, 10.

As shown in the diagram, the cards in any one row may be mixed up, just so they contain the requisite denominations to complete your key.

The cards used in the layout may be of any suits, as it is denomination only that is significant. If you are told that the card chosen is not represented on the table, you know they must be thinking of the joker.

The Patter:

I have here a portion of a pack of cards—twenty-eight to be exact—which I shall deal on the table in four rows, these cards acting as a chart. By using this chart and with a little concentration, it is my intention to learn the denomination of any card you may think of. There are the completed rows, and that I may not be accused of detecting your card from their order I will turn my back while you are making a selection.

Mr. ———, will you kindly select mentally any card in the pack? It makes no difference whether it is on the table or not. You have one? Just think of it for a moment. And would you mind telling me if you see a card of your denomination in the first row? It is? How about the second row, is it also there? The third row? Not present? And it is in the fourth row? Yes? Thank you. Will you tell me the suit of the card you thought of? Spades? Spades; just a second. Just concentrate on it. The jack—jack of spades. Correct? (*Continue, if desired, detecting further selections in the same manner.*)

THE FORTUNE-TELLING JACK.

This is without doubt the most deceptive and puzzling of the entire category of card effects not requiring sleight-of-hand, but its effectiveness depends to a large extent upon the manner of presentation.

Any cards can be used, the effect being heightened by using a borrowed deck.

The effect: You borrow a pack of cards from your host or hostess, first requesting that they be thoroughly shuffled. Another person cuts the cards near the center of the deck. You take one half and he takes the other, and each one counts his own portion. Several cards are then drawn by members of the audience, and are put in various places out of sight so that no one is aware of which cards they are. Upon placing the jack of spades, which you remove from the pack, near these cards, he apparently whispers to you the name of each individual one, for you announce the number and suit of the hidden card which is found correct in each case.

The method: The only requisite is your ability to memorize quickly from three to five cards in a given order.

Borrow a pack and say that you will remove the jack of spades. In seeking the card you naturally hold the face of the pack toward yourself. You fan the bottom cards slightly, and while locating the jack you memorize several cards at the bottom of the pack, starting with the last one, which for convenience we will say are the ace, two, three and four of hearts. Remove the jack of spades and lay it to one side. Place the pack on the table and request that it be cut. You allow the cutter to retain his half of the pack and you take the lower half. Have this person count his cards. You do likewise with yours, dealing them down on the table one at a time, face down, as you count. This reverses their position. When the counting is finished place your half on top of the other and square the deck. The top card of the pack is now the ace of hearts, followed by the two, three and four. In other words, the cards you noted at the bottom of the pack are, due to reversal in counting, now in the same order at the top of the pack.

You request that a card be selected and hid under a book, placed in some one's pocket or otherwise concealed, holding out the pack and slightly pushing off the top card. Should a person hesitate about taking this card, simply move on to the next one. They do not know what you are going to do, and have not the slightest idea that you are familiar with the position of any of the cards. Having passed out as many cards as you memorized, pick up the jack and hold it near where the first card is secreted. Then hold it to your ear and state that the jack announces this card is the ace of hearts, and so on.

On paper, the effect may not look so promising, but after a trial the results will be more than satisfactory.

The Patter:

May I borrow a pack of your cards, Madam? I want to illustrate a lesson witnessed by myself last week; one demonstrating that inanimate objects have the power of thought transmission. I presume this appears to you like a foolhardy statement, but let the result speak for itself. Thank you for the cards. But first will you kindly shuffle them thoroughly? That will do nicely.

I desire to remove the jack of spades from the pack, as it is the chief factor in this drama, or whatever you desire to term it. (*Remove the jack and sight the bottom cards.*) And you, sir, kindly cut the cards somewhere near the center, and count your half down on the table. I will do likewise with these. (*For instance:*) Twenty-three? And I have here twenty-nine, making fifty-two, which makes the pack complete. (*Or, in case the pack is short, say only forty-nine cards being therein.*) Forty-nine? Well, that will be sufficient for our experiment.

I am now going to ask several of you to each remove a card from the pack. But don't look at it, and don't let anyone else see it. And above all things, don't let me catch a glimpse of your card. As soon as you take the card place it out of sight—under the table drape, in your pocket, in the leaves of a book, or anywhere you may choose. Will you have one?

Just hide it. That's right. And will you accommodate me? (*Talk along these lines until the known cards have been distributed.*)

Here is the jack of spades, which I previously removed. He represents the court jester, or fool—but, far from being a fool, he is the wisest card in the pack, and he is going to communicate to me the names of the various members of his family you have hidden. (*Place jack near concealed card and then hold to ear.*)

The jack tells me that this card is a red one—a heart—the ace of hearts. Kindly look and see if that is correct. It is? You see the jack is not only possessed of wisdom, but has keen eyesight as well. Now, jack, this card here! He says this is also a heart—one with two spots. Therefore, it must be a deuce of hearts. Is he correct? Yes, that's right; he seldom errs. (*Proceed until the others have been located.*)

THE CARD TO THE POCKET.

Here is an easy and practical method of performing a popular effect which heretofore has depended on great skill in sleight-of-hand.

The effect: A spectator takes a pack of cards in his hands, shuffles them, counts down a few cards from the top of the deck, and notes the number and suit of the card at that location. The performer then takes the pack, holds it behind his back, and removes a card, which he places in his pocket, announcing that it is the one chosen. The pack is again handed to the spectator, who is asked how many cards down he counted. He is then asked to count down to that number and see if the card is there. On being informed that it is not, the performer remarks that it couldn't be, for he placed it in his pocket, whence he removes the card, and shows it to be correct.

The method: This is a simplified procedure that does away with palming, and at the same time heightens the effect. After the spectator has counted down a certain number, which is done while your back is turned, take the pack from him. When it is placed behind your back you take off ten or twelve cards, holding them tightly together, and place them quickly in your pocket, not allowing the face card to be seen. Apparently you have drawn and pocketed one card only. It rarely happens that a person will count down more than six or seven cards, but this can be judged well enough by the time he takes in counting. Hand the pack back, asking at what number the card was. Your hand now goes into your pocket and you count down the given number of cards while the spectator is looking for his card. Of course it is not now in the deck, but in your pocket. After he finds it is not in the deck, take the card clear from your pocket and exhibit as the one chosen. Hold the pack with the backs upward when taking off the cards, put them in your pocket with their faces toward your body, and count down the given number from the top.

The Patter:

I claim to be a mind reader, as far as the cards are concerned. If you will take the pack and follow my directions you can judge for yourself. While I turn my back count down a few cards from the top, not disturbing their present position, though you may shuffle them if you desire before starting. When you have counted down a few then look at the card, remembering what card it is, and also do not forget its position in the pack. Have you done so? Kindly allow me to have the pack, which I will place behind my back. Without asking you a single question I will remove your card and place it in my pocket, which I believe will cause you to agree with my statement so far as mind reading is concerned.

There is the pack. May I ask at what number your card was? The seventh? Count down and see if it is now in the seventh position. No? It is not? I know it. It couldn't be, because here it is in my pocket. The name, please? Six of spades. Correct. The six of spades. (*Turn face up and exhibit.*)

THE GUESSER.

Here is a puzzling experiment in which from four to seven spectators may participate at one time. It is particularly useful in entertaining at parlor gatherings, where all present may be invited to "assist."

The effect: After allowing the deck to be thoroughly shuffled, the performer fans out a few cards and shows them to a spectator, who mentally selects a card. The process is repeated several times, showing a different fan to each spectator. When each has thus noted a card in a fan, the cards are disarranged so that they form fans of different combinations. Simply showing each of the new fans to each of the persons in turn and learning whether their card is in the fan, without the performer looking at the faces of the cards, he "guesses" the ones chosen, and at the conclusion of the experiment the cards which he has "guessed" to be the ones chosen are proven to be correct.

The method: Although you do not call attention to the fact, each fan is made up of the same number of cards as there are people on whom you work the trick. Not less than four people should be used, and of course it cannot be done with more than seven, as that would require forty-nine cards and there are only fifty-two in the deck. We will assume that six spectators are participating.

After allowing the deck to be freely shuffled, you take up the first six, without seeming intentionally to select that number, and hold them up before the first party, whom we will call "A." You do not look at the faces of the cards yourself now or at any other time in the course of the experiment. Fanning the six cards, you ask A to mentally note one of them. Close the fan and lay it face downward on the table. Fan out the next six cards for B, and when he has mentally selected one, lay this stack of six next to the first six. Continue in the same way until A, B, C, D, E and F have each noted a card from a different group of cards, and you have the six groups in a row on the table, face downward. Lay aside the rest of the deck, as you will not use it again.

Now stack the six groups together in regular order, with first group on top and last at the bottom. Remarking that you will disarrange them to make different combinations, lay out the top six (which formerly made up one fan) one at a time, then lay six more on top of them, and so on, until you have made six fresh stacks. Each of the original fans is now represented by some one card in each of the six new groups, the original first group being represented by the bottom card, the next by the second card, and so on.

Pick up the first pile, fan them and ask A if his card is in this new fan. If he says yes, you know it must be the bottom card. Whether his reply is affirmative or negative, show this same fan to B and ask him if his card is present. If it is, it must be the next to the bottom card. Show this fan to each of the six in turn. A's card, if present, must be at the bottom; B's card must be next to the bottom; C's card third from the bottom, and so on to F's, which must be the top card of whatever group it is in.

Remember, you do not ask them the location. You simply ask if their card is in the fan. Perhaps none of the chosen cards are in the fan. Perhaps several are present. But when the answer is in the affirmative, you know immediately which card it is, by the rotation of the cards in the fan. If all say "No," lay this fan aside and fan out the next six. But we will assume that A and D say "Yes." You know A's card must be at the bottom, and D's must be third from the top. Hold the fan behind your back and take out these two, laying A's card face downward in an imaginary first position on the table, and D's in an imaginary fourth position, so that when all six have been located they will lie in a row.

Repeat the process with the remaining cards, showing them in fans six at a time, and showing each fan to each of the six spectators. Thus you locate each of the six cards, "guessing" at them behind your back whenever a chosen card is reported present in the fan, and laying each chosen card, face downward, in its place in the row on the table.

You finally have six cards in a row. Asking A what his card was, and having his reply, you turn over the first card, which is his. Repeat with the other five. So, without having asked any questions as to location, etc., and without seeing the faces at any time, you have apparently selected each of the mentally selected cards. Since this trick requires neither sleight-of-hand skill nor any preparation of the pack, it is highly recommended as an impromptu experiment for the amateur.

The Patter:

While I have the cards I will take up a few more minutes of your time to demonstrate that sometimes it is possible to accomplish a good deal by guesswork. Please shuffle the cards thoroughly, and you will notice that I do not see the faces of the cards at any time during the experiment. Thank you.

Mrs. A———, will you kindly make a mental note of one card in this fan? And please don't forget it. Mr. B———, will you likewise remember any one of the cards in this second fan? Choose any one, but keep the number and suit of your chosen card carefully in mind. Miss C———, I will ask you to make a choice from this third fan, in the same way; any card at all. It makes no difference. Mrs. D———, will you please make a choice, the same as the others have done? You will notice that I do not ask you to draw a card, or even to touch them, so I have no way of knowing what card of the fifty-two you are selecting. Mr. E———, will you oblige in the same way? And, finally, Mr. F———, when you have noted a card in the last fan we will proceed.

Bear in mind that I have given you (*stack the six fans for the re-deal*) a perfectly free choice in each instance. But to relieve any suspicion that I might perhaps know what card you selected by your glance, I will further mix the cards by dealing them out in separate heaps which, as you can readily see, changes their positions throughout.

Once again I shall exhibit these new individual

fans. And, as I display each of them to all of you, all I ask is that you tell me whether or not your card is in the fan. (*Showing a new fan.*) Mrs. A———, does your card appear amongst these? Don't tell me the card, or its position in the fan. It does? I thank you. Placing the fan behind my back, my guess is (*remove bottom card from fan and place on table, face downward*) that this is your card. Mr. B———, is your card present? No? And you, Miss C———? And how about you, Mrs. D———? Yes? Then I will make another guess, and pick out this one. (*Remove card and lay on table as before. Continue with remaining cards until all chosen have been "guessed."*)

I have made six guesses, and I have selected the six cards now on the table as the ones chosen. And you will remember that I have asked no questions as to the identity of your cards, nor their location in the fans, nor have I seen the faces of the cards at any time. Now, Mrs. A———, as a matter of verification, kindly tell me the name of your card. (*She replies, for instance, "The ten of diamonds."*) The ten of diamonds? (*Turn over first card.*) Well, I guessed right that time. I believe you will find the remaining guesses equally good. Your card, Mr. B———? The four of clubs? (*Turn over second card, and so on, until all are shown.*)

THE LEMON AND DOLLAR BILL TRICK.

This highly popular effect has been presented with great success in vaudeville for some years. In the present version the disagreeable features and the necessity for any degree of skill have been eliminated, without detracting from the effectiveness.

The effect: A dollar bill is borrowed and placed in an envelope, which is sealed and given to a boy from audience, with instructions to burn the envelope. While he is performing this task you exhibit two lemons, go among the audience and have one selected, leaving the other as a souvenir. Returning to the platform or end of the room, inquire of the boy whether he burned the envelope. Then ask him for the dollar bill. When he confesses the money was burned with the envelope, the lemon is cut open and the bill is found therein and returned to its owner.

The method: On the small table or stand which you use for your "properties," or articles employed, is a book or a cigar box, on top of which is an ordinary envelope containing a piece of stage paper money; or any slip of green paper will do that at a glance resembles a folded bill. Of the two lemons used, one is unfaked. The other has a hole punched lengthwise with a pencil or small stick, through one end and more than half way through the lemon.

In preparing this lemon, jab the stick around to make a fair-sized hole. Then squeeze the lemon to rid it of part of the juice. Take a dollar bill, first making a note of its serial number, roll it up small and insert it in the lemon. Don't use a brand new dollar bill, nor a badly worn one. The rest of the "props" consist of a saucer, a small bottle of wood alcohol, and a few matches. Before starting, memorize the last two or three numbers of the bill that is in the lemon; or the entire number may be written on your thumb nail. These preparations are all made, of course, secretly and in advance.

Begin the experiment by borrowing a dollar bill.

If possible, obtain one of the same style as the one in the lemon. Only three styles of dollar bills are made, most of them being the ones with the eagle on the back, or the one with the large cross. If you cannot obtain the desired type, however, the difference in style will not be noticed. Avoid accepting a new bill or a bill that is badly frayed, if you can, for while the one from the lemon will be wet, a brand new one can be told from a worn article.

As soon as you receive the bill, ask the lender to remember its number, not allowing him to see it, but you yourself reading off to him the entire number, or the last two numerals. Of course you look at the bill, but you really quote the numbers of your own bill, not his. Fold up this borrowed bill rather small, pick up the envelope from the table, and in the act of so doing allow the borrowed bill to fall behind the book or box on the table, while apparently placing it inside the envelope.

Get a boy from the audience to assist you and, just before sealing, take the fake bill out of the envelope and immediately replace it. Seal the envelope and instruct the boy to burn it.

Pick up the lemons from the table, holding one in either hand, and resting the tampered end against the ball of the thumb so it will appear to be an ordinary lemon. "Force" the unfaked lemon as shown in the patter. Returning to the boy, ask him for the bill. Then cut open the faked lemon, making the incision near the center and of course holding the open end away from the audience. When the lemon is cut in two the bill should adhere to the good end, if it has been shoved far enough into the lemon, so the open end may be thrown aside on the table.

The Patter:

Not being a regular magician, I do not carry my own apparatus. Therefore, I am forced to borrow. In this instance I would like to borrow a dollar bill— a second-hand one will do just as well as a new one. I haven't any of my own. And I'd rather take a chance with yours, anyway. (*If a brand new bill is offered you*:) Thank you, sir, but I hate to take such a nice, crisp new bill from a man on payday, when I don't know what's going to happen to it. Haven't you a bill that wouldn't mind a few hard knocks? (*Or, if bill offered is too badly worn*:) This one is pretty far gone. I really hate to be responsible for it, because I might not be able to save the pieces. How about one with a little more endurance?

A kind-hearted gentleman who thinks I look honest lends me a dollar—without interest. See how easy it is when you know how. Making the "buck" into small change. (*Fold once.*) Four bits. (*Fold again.*) Two bits, which we will deposit—not in a bank but in this envelope, leaving it here for a few minutes.

Now, then, I want to borrow a boy. Young man, will you come up and help me? That's right. I'm perfectly harmless. Thank you. What's your name, Johnnie? (*Keep on calling him "Johnnie," regardless of his name.*) All right, Johnnie, I'm going to let you hold this money. Just hold it—that's all. How does it feel to be a capitalist? Do me another favor. Here is a saucer, on the saucer is the envelope, and to facilitate the action I will add a little alcohol. Follow my instructions carefully: Take this match, place the saucer over on that stand, and burn the envelope, while I visit the audience again. (*Take up lemons.*)

Quite a curiosity, two imported lemons. Yes, they are; I got them from abroad. Any good judges of lemons present? Will you, little girl, choose one of these? This one? I thank you, we will use the one you selected. You can have the other for a souvenir. You might call that handing you a lemon, but I don't mean it in that way. (*Or if they choose the unprepared one.*) All right, you may keep it as a souvenir. I'll use the one remaining.

Here we are, Johnnie. Did you burn the envelope? You did? Make a good job of it? Fine! Let me have the dollar bill, please. What's that? You burned it? I didn't tell you to burn the bill. I said to burn the envelope. That money belongs to the gentleman over there. (*This argument may be short-ened or lengthened to suit the occasion and the type of audience.*)

What are we going to do about it? Have you a dollar? No? Neither have I. You'll surely have to help me now. Hold the saucer containing the ashes over your head, close your left eye, look sharply at the lemon, and say, real loud: "Lemon, lemon"—no, we've had enough lemons hanging around. Say, "Dollar, dollar, hop into the lemon!" That's the way. If you are a good magician perhaps we saved ourselves some money. Let's see.

I believe you did it. Our magic worked. There's something in the lemon. Yes, it's a dollar. You take it back to the man. Wring it out first if you want to. Make yourself some lemonade.

BURLESQUE MIND READING.

In the presentation of the following comedy act, for those who are willing to expend a little time and money, the outfitting of the "Prince" in befitting uniform or costume will add considerable mystery and amusement.

This act can be presented in the parlor, at clubs, or at any character of social or community gatherings, either by two men or by a man and a woman.

It seems hardly necessary to say that if the act is started off in all seriousness, the attention of your audience will be more centered, and the direct cueing of the first one or two questions will not be noticeable. Various questions and answers can be worked out along these lines to suit the occasion. Keep the questions and answers going in rapid-fire fashion.

In the dialogue, the questions asked by the "professor" in the audience, and his remarks, are designed by the letter "Q." The replies of the "Prince" are preceded by the letter "A."

The Patter:

Ladies and gentlemen: It is with great pleasure this evening that I introduce to you the world's greatest master of thought transference—a man with a brain of such mental magnitude and wonderful development that the slightest thought is instantly transmitted and registered in his mind—the man to whom the ordinary human brain is like an open book. During our experiments I have to request that you remain as quiet as possible, in order that the proper psychic conditions may prevail. Ladies and gentlemen—Prince Sapolio! (*The "Prince" enters.*)

I shall now attempt to verify the truth of my assertions, convincing even the most skeptical. I shall

pass down among you, allowing those who so desire
to ask a question of any nature, or to hand me articles of various kinds. The Prince will immediately
and correctly answer such questions or describe the
designated objects.

In order to relieve suspicion that any signals are
employed, or that the Prince might catch a glimpse
of the articles, I shall first securely blindfold him.
(*Seat the "Prince" in chair and blindfold him, facing
the audience. Don't give persons a chance to really
ask any questions. Invent them as you go along.*)
Are you ready, Prince? All right.

Q.—Don't let me stick you. What's this?

A.—A stick pin.

Q.—Quite correct.

Q.—What has this man on his head?

A.—Hair.

Q.—Correct again.

Q.—What has this party on his feet?

A.—Shoes.

Q.—Marvellous. Now, tell me, is this a male or
female?

A.—You mean whether it is a man or woman?

Q.—Yes. Is *he* a man or a woman?

A.—A man.

Q.—Fine, fine.

Q.—Look *here,* what is this?

A.—An ear.

Q.—Right you are. How many ears has the little
boy?

A.—Two.

Q.—Right again. Now, what's the matter with his
ears?

A.—They need washing.

Q.—Once more ; tell me the color of this lady's hair. Hurry up.   This is a hot one.

A.—Red.

Q.—Correct.   The Prince never fails.

Q.—A lady desires to know when the two-forty-five train leaves for ———— (*nearby town*)?

A.—At fifteen minutes to three.

Q.—Absolutely correct.

Q.—Watch out, now.   What is this?

A.—A watch.

Q.—Very good.   Tell me what kind of watch it is?

A.—It's a Jewish watch.

Q.—A Jewish watch?   How do you make that out?

A.—Because its hands are always moving.

Q.—A gentlemen hands me a coin.   Can you tell me the value of this four-bit piece?

A.—Yes, I can.   Fifty cents.

Q.—What has this man around his neck?

A.—A necktie.

Q.—You are doing fine, Prince.

Q.—How many fingers is the lady holding up? Hurry up.   I don't want to ask you over three times.

A.—Three.

Q.—Not so good.

Q.—Prince, tell me: What is this gentleman's occupation?

A.—That gentleman is a carpenter.

Q.—A carpenter?   How do you make that out?

A.—Because he has two bits in his pocket.

Q.—And this gentleman's occupation?

A.—He is a fruit specialist.

Q.—And what makes you think that?

A.—Look at the "peach" he has with him.

Q.—That's right. Tell me what this man does.

A.—That man is a florist.

Q.—I don't see how you figure that out.

A.—Haven't you noticed him eyeing up the "daisies" all evening?

Q.—All right, Prince. I know you never make mistakes, so tell me what this gentleman does for a living.

A.—He is an electrician.

Q.—Your reason for such assertion?

A.—I can read his mind and his thoughts shock me.

Q.—Hurry up, Prince. How much money has this young lady in her pocketbook?

A.—The young lady has 63 cents in her pocketbook—but that isn't all the money she has with her.

Q.—Listen. What is on this lady's finger?

A.—A ring.

Q.—Right you are. What kind of a ring has this married lady?

A.—A wedding ring.

Q.—This young man says he is going to give his girl a present for her birthday. Tell me what it is.

A.—I don't seem to get that.

Q.—Come on—a present—something for her neck.

A.—Oh! A bar of soap.

Q.—What has this young lady in her hand?

A.—Her sweetheart's hand—or she did have, a moment ago.

Q.—Now, as a supreme test of the Prince's unfailing accuracy, I am going to ask some person in the back of the hall to remove a coin from his pocket, look at the date, and keep the coin securely out of sight. (*In the meantime you return to the platform.*) Prince, a gentleman in the back of the hall is holding in his hand a coin. Will you tell me the date?

A.—August 1st, 19—. (*Mention the day of the month and year of your entertainment.*)

BODY AND HAT LOADING.

As the average beginner in magic generally wishes to be able to extract articles from a borrowed hat or from the person of a voluntary assistant, and as this is always an amusing stunt, suitable for all occasions, and easy of execution, it is explained herewith in order that the beginner may create comedy upon the completion of some of the tricks previously explained.

If a person has been assisting you in a card trick reach under his coat before dismissing him and procure a number of cards. This is accomplished by what the card manipulator terms "palming." If a pack of cards be held in the right hand, thumb on one end and fingers on the other, so that the entire pack is covered with the hand, and the pack is then transferred to the left hand, which riffles the cards before taking actual hold of them, this riffling will cause a number of the top cards to spring up against the palm of the right hand, where they can be retained by a slight contraction. The right hand is immediately inserted under the volunteer's coat and the cards are produced fanwise to make the production seem greater. Again, the cards may be tucked up close to the volunteer's armpit under the coat, where they will remain without falling. The performer "finds" only one card, leaving the balance "planted." From this position they may then be produced one at a time.

While attention is being drawn to this removal of cards with the right hand, your left hand may obtain from under the vest any small collapsible article, such as a string of sausages, colored silk handkerchiefs, etc., and these deliberately removed and likewise inserted under the volunteer's coat, to be produced in their turn.

When a performer removes larger objects, such as live stock, etc., it is accomplished in the following manner: The articles are concealed in a large pocket in the left-hand inner side of your coat. After "finding" some small articles, such as cards, in a spectator's clothing, ask him if he has anything else concealed about his person, at the same time turning him around so his back is toward the audience, and telling him in an undertone to hold his coat open, this acting as a shield to your movements. Stand up close to him, bringing your "load" out of your inner coat pocket with your right hand and quickly getting it into position under his opened coat. Have him release his coat, then reach down back of his neck under his coat, and pull out whatever you have just "planted" therein.

Loading articles into a hat can be accomplished in various ways. It is well to practice hat loading and body loading before a mirror, in order that the proper angles may be obtained.

A load into a hat may be achieved by any of the following methods:

Under your vest have a few handkerchiefs that are

rolled up tightly into a ball. Borrow a hat. Show it back and front. Then, when the crown is toward the audience, bring the hat close to your body. Under its cover secure the vest load, and drop it into the hat.

The load may be hanging back of your table by a fine wire that is looped and is pinned at the top of the table. Show the hat empty and hit the brim lightly on the table, immediately over where load is hanging. Your first finger engages in the loop and draws up the load so it can be tilted into the hat.

The load can be hanging on a thread and hung out about a foot behind your table by means of a small stick fastened thereto. In passing behind the table, the hat scoops up the load, breaking the thread. The hat is at once tilted so the contents cannot be seen. This method of loading may also be accomplished by using a solid-backed chair instead of a table.

After you have introduced a small load of silk handkerchiefs into a hat, additional articles may be dumped in after taking out the load, by laying the produced articles down on the table, getting hold of the second load hung on the back of table and apparently showing that the silks fill the hat, placing the first articles back therein, and at the same time introducing the second load, which is hidden by the silks.

If you are using your own hat, try this. Cut off the brim of an old black derby hat and insert the bowl or crown in another hat. Have this inserted hat come to within a couple of inches of the top of the crown of the good derby, leaving between the two crowns a space sufficient for storing quite a number of silk handkerchiefs. This inserted bowl should be slit crosswise, so that the fingers can reach thereunder and take hold of the handkerchiefs inside the partition. In using a hat of this character it can be shown from all sides, the hand being inserted without a false move, and a number of silks produced. Additional loads may be secured from the table under cover of the first production.

PALMING

In the repertoire of tricks which have been herein explained the necessity for specialized skill, or actual sleight-of-hand, has been practically eliminated. However, a fundamental knowledge of palming is desired by even the beginner in magic, and this knowledge, after some practice, can often be used to enhance the effect in presenting some small pocket trick, as well as being essential to further advance in the art.

Palming is the foundation of sleight-of-hand, be it with cards, coins, billiard balls or other small objects. To palm means to conceal in the hand, unnoticed by the audience, any small article that is being used by the conjurer.

Palming is a difficult task, in one sense, yet it is not nearly so difficult as is imagined by the uninformed. The trouble with the average beginner is that when he tries to palm an article he cramps his hand to an unnecessary degree. And even when he has mastered the correct position, he is painfully conscious of the fact that he is palming an article and he imagines that the audience is also aware of it. With this self-consciousness, proper misdirection is impossible.

The actual holding of the article in the hand is the least part of palming. The real art is in retaining the article naturally while the other hand is performing some duty to divert the attention of the audience, thus giving the necessary misdirection.

For example, let us assume that you have a billiard ball which is to vanish from the left hand and be found in the right-hand trousers pocket. You pick up the ball with your right hand and apparently place it in the left hand. In reality you push it down into the palm of the right hand, out of sight of the audience (see Figure 19), while the left hand

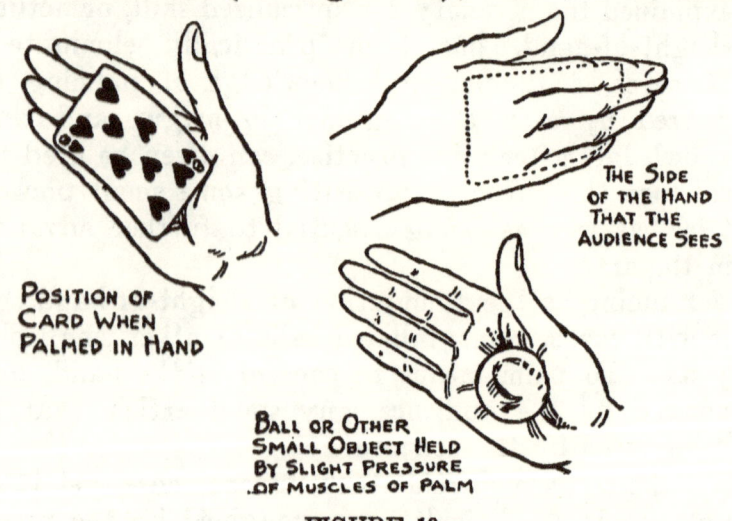

POSITION OF
CARD WHEN
PALMED IN HAND

THE SIDE
OF THE HAND
THAT THE
AUDIENCE SEES

BALL OR OTHER
SMALL OBJECT HELD
BY SLIGHT PRESSURE
OF MUSCLES OF PALM

FIGURE 19

closes as if containing the ball and moves away from the right hand. If this move is properly made, the eyes of the spectators will follow the left hand, thinking it contains the ball, and the right hand will lose their attention. You should aid the misdirection by holding your left hand in exactly the position that it would take if it really contained the ball, and fixing your own attention on it, absolutely ignoring your right hand wherein the ball is palmed.

Now you squeeze your left hand slowly as though
the ball is vanishing into thin air, and explaining
that the ball which has just been seen to vanish
from the left hand has travelled invisibly into
the trousers pocket, you casually reach into your
pocket with your right hand, introducing the palmed
ball therein and immediately bringing it forth, holding it between your finger tips.

This is just one example of the function of palming, but it serves to bring out the point to be em-
phasized. That is, the performer must pay absolutely no heed to the hand wherein the object is
palmed. He must carry out the idea that it is held
in the other hand, or otherwise misdirect the attention of the spectators if the object has been secretly
palmed for the purpose of producing later in any
manner. Do not look at the palming hand, and do
not cramp it unnecessarily. These precautions are
essential to misdirection in palming.

Applying the art of palming to cards, let us assume that you wish to secretly remove the top card
from the deck. Hold the pack in the right hand,
with the thumb at one end of the pack and the
fingers at the other. Transfer the pack to the left
hand, which takes it with the fingers underneath
and the thumb on top. In taking the pack, the
thumb of the left hand slips the top card sidewise
(or endwise, if more convenient) far enough for the
right hand to take hold of it by slightly contract-
ing. With the top card thus secretly removed and
palmed in the right hand (see Figure 19), the left
hand moves away with the pack while the right hand
is dropped casually at the side. The pack can now
be "riffled" with the left hand and the card produced

from the knee with the right hand, or the palmed card may be "found" in any manner that the experiment requires. If it is desired to produce a fan of cards, several cards instead of one are shoved up into the palm at the moment of transferring the pack, and they may be produced from the elbow or out of the air. By spreading them fanwise at the moment of producing them, a few cards will appear to be a very large handful.

Figure 19 will give a general idea of the principle of palming. In each case of course the back of the hand is supposed to be toward the audience. Always bear in mind that the hand should not be contracted any more than is necessary to retain the object, and should not appear cramped. Neither should the hand be stretched out stiff nor the fingers widely separated, as this is equally sure to cause suspicion.

The best way to study palming is to practice in front of a mirror. If you are going to palm a ball in the right hand while seeming to take it in the left, actually make the transfer first and study the position of the hands. Then perform the palm and fake transfer, simulating the natural positions as you have observed them. Pretend to yourself, just as you will pretend to the audience, that the palming hand is empty. And never forget that in palming or in any other branch of sleight-of-hand, adroitness or skill in itself is not enough. Beside dexterity, you need perfect ease and self-assurance, and these come only with practice and experience.

And now the author makes his bow, with the hope that this book will be the means of enabling many a beginner in magic to acquire that selfsame practice and experience without having first to serve a long apprenticeship before appearing in public. Skill and dexterity in real sleight-of-hand should come all the more easily for having mastered these easy effects in IMPROMPTU MAGIC, WITH PATTER.

FINIS.